DEVELOPING DIGITAL A...

Social Media and the News

Carla Mooney

San Diego, CA

About the Author

Carla Mooney is the author of many books for young adults and children. She lives in Pittsburgh, Pennsylvania, with her husband and three children.

© 2024 ReferencePoint Press, Inc.
Printed in the United States

For more information, contact:
ReferencePoint Press, Inc.
PO Box 27779
San Diego, CA 92198
www.ReferencePointPress.com

ALL RIGHTS RESERVED.
No part of this work covered by the copyright hereon may be reproduced or used in any form or by any means—graphic, electronic, or mechanical, including photocopying, recording, taping, web distribution, or information storage retrieval systems—without the written permission of the publisher.

LIBRARY OF CONGRESS CATALOGING-IN-PUBLICATION DATA

Names: Mooney, Carla, 1970- author.
Title: Social media and the news / by Carla Mooney.
Description: San Diego, CA : ReferencePoint Press, 2024. | Series: Developing digital and media literacy skills | Includes bibliographical references and index.
Identifiers: LCCN 2023009458 (print) | LCCN 2023009459 (ebook) | ISBN 9781678205386 (library binding) | ISBN 9781678205393 (ebook)
Subjects: LCSH: Social media--Juvenile literature. | Online social networks--Juvenile literature. | Misinformation--Juvenile literature. | Disinformation--Juvenile literature. | Fake news--Juvenile literature.
Classification: LCC HM742 .M663 2024 (print) | LCC HM742 (ebook) | DDC 302.23/1--dc23/eng/20230405
LC record available at https://lccn.loc.gov/2023009458
LC ebook record available at https://lccn.loc.gov/2023009459

CONTENTS

Introduction — 4
Distributing News on TikTok

Chapter One — 8
How People Get News

Chapter Two — 17
False and Misleading Information Goes Viral

Chapter Three — 26
Social Media Creates Echo Chambers

Chapter Four — 35
Evaluating News Sources

Chapter Five — 47
Recognizing Bias

Source Notes	56
For Further Research	59
Index	61
Picture Credits	64

INTRODUCTION

Distributing News on TikTok

In March 2022 the White House invited thirty leading TikTok influencers for a virtual meeting. White House press secretary Jen Psaki and staffers from the National Security Council spoke to the influencers about Russia's invasion of Ukraine. The government officials briefed the influencers about the United States' strategic goals in eastern Europe. They answered questions on several topics, including aid to Ukraine, the US partnership with the North Atlantic Treaty Organization, and how the United States planned to respond if Russia used nuclear weapons. The briefing was an extraordinary acknowledgment of social media's growing role in distributing news in modern society. "We recognize this is a critically important avenue in the way the American public is finding out about the latest, so we wanted to make sure you had the latest information from an authoritative source,"[1] White House director of digital strategy Rob Flaherty said in the meeting.

TikTok is a popular social media platform that allows users to create, share, and watch short videos on cell phones or other mobile devices. While TikTok is best known for its user-submitted videos of dances, pranks, stunts, jokes, and other tricks, the social media platform has also become a place for users to get news and information. As the Ukraine-Russia conflict escalated, millions worldwide turned to TikTok to get real-time information about what was happening in Ukraine. Ukrainian people shared video stories of hiding in bomb shelters or evacuating their homes. At the same time, false information, some of which was deliberately spread by Russian sources, appeared on the platform.

> "People in my generation get all our information from TikTok. It's the first place we're searching up new topics and learning about things."[2]
>
> —Kahlil Greene, twenty-one-year-old TikTok influencer

Aware of TikTok's rise as a place to find news, the Biden administration worked with the nonprofit advocacy group Gen-Z for Change to identify top TikTok content creators and invite them to the virtual meeting about the Russia-Ukraine conflict. Kahlil Greene, a twenty-one-year-old with more than 534,000 TikTok followers, was one of the influencers invited to the virtual meeting. "People in my generation get all our information from TikTok. It's the first place we're searching up new topics and learning about things,"[2] he says.

Social Media's Influence

The US government has increasingly turned to influential social media users to spread the word about major policy initiatives. For example, the Biden administration has worked with dozens

TikTok's users can view, share, and create short videos on their smartphones. Increasingly, though, people are using TikTok as a source of news and information.

> "There's a massive cultural and generational shift happening in media, and you have to have blinders on not to see it. The reach of a piece in a traditional news outlet is a fraction of what a big TikToker gets."[3]
>
> —Teddy Goff, cofounder of Precision Strategies, a consulting firm

of TikTok influencers on several issues, including vaccines and infrastructure. "There's a massive cultural and generational shift happening in media, and you have to have blinders on not to see it. The reach of a piece in a traditional news outlet is a fraction of what a big TikToker gets,"[3] says Teddy Goff, cofounder of the consulting firm Precision Strategies.

Hours after the March 2022 meeting, the TikTokers posted messages to their followers. One of those influencers is eighteen-year-old Ellie Zeiler, who has more than 10.5 million followers. She hopes to continue informing followers about essential news items. Zeiler sees herself as providing valuable information to the growing number of people who get their news primarily on social media platforms. "I'm here to relay the information in a more digestible manner to my followers. I would consider myself a White House correspondent for Gen Z,"[4] she says.

More than a Place to Socialize

Although social media platforms started as a place to socialize online, for people worldwide social media has increasingly become a source for news. According to a 2022 Pew Research Center study, approximately 70 percent of Americans get at least some news from social media platforms. News information comes directly from posts by traditional news sources such as broadcast and cable news outlets, newsmagazines, and newspapers. Other news content comes from alternative news sources and sometimes from platform users.

Teens and young adults in particular are turning to social media for news. According to the aforementioned Pew Research Center study, adults under age thirty make up the largest share of people who get news on social media sites. Among the most popular sites for news, according to the Pew Research Center study, are Facebook, YouTube, Twitter, Instagram, TikTok, and Reddit.

People turn to social media for news for a variety reasons. Some platforms, like Twitter, are a good place to get breaking news and updates. "When I'm wondering what is going on in the world . . . Twitter [is] definitely like the first place I go to, and usually there's like a news story that's breaking, and I can read the news and read people's opinions,"[5] says a twenty-one-year-old American woman who participated in a 2021 Reuters Institute survey on social media and news.

People also turn to social media for news because of the interaction and convenience these platforms provide. Some people enjoy the interactive nature of social media platforms, where they can comment and debate with other users about current events and issues. For others, getting news on social media is simple; users can quickly search to find news topics that interest them. And for many, finding news on social media is also convenient. They are already on the platforms for other reasons and see news posts as they scroll through their social media feeds. "Nowadays where I see news most is on Facebook, because that's when you are . . . already seeing photos, things you like,"[6] says a twenty-eight-year-old woman from Brazil.

A Complicated Relationship

Concerns have risen as more people turn to social media for news. While some information on social media platforms comes from trustworthy news outlets, other news sources are unreliable, misleading, and inaccurate. When fact, opinion, bias, and misinformation are all jumbled together on a social media platform, it is not surprising that users can have trouble determining what they are seeing.

CHAPTER ONE

How People Get News

Before social media platforms emerged, most people got their news from traditional outlets such as newspapers, television news programs, and radio shows. Traditional news outlets and the journalists who worked for them controlled the stories they reported to the public and decided what articles to print or stories to air. Most of the time, the general public could rely on the accuracy of the news these outlets reported because the news organizations and journalists were responsible for fact-checking information in their stories and ensuring they used truthful, accurate sources before publishing them.

Under this model of news reporting, the average person had little input into what stories appeared in the news and how they were covered. The public read, watched, and listened to news stories and rarely had the chance to engage and participate in news reporting. However, the rapid embrace of social media by people worldwide has opened up a new pathway for people to get their news.

Social Media's Rising Popularity

In less than twenty years, social media has exploded in popularity worldwide. In 2005 only 5 percent of American adults used at least one social media platform, according to the Pew Research Center. By 2011 half of American adults were on social media; by 2023 nearly three-quarters of the public used some form of social media.

At first, social media connected users with friends, family, and people with similar interests online. Users joined online communities from desktop and laptop computers and socialized with others without leaving home. With the introduction of smartphones, social media went mobile. And as smartphone cameras became more powerful, social media users could upload images and video, along with text.

Social media platforms such as Facebook, Twitter, Snapchat, Instagram, and TikTok have thrived on mobile devices. Users can take their online communities wherever they go, posting, commenting, and uploading content from anywhere. Businesses have taken advantage of the growing number of people on social media by creating social profiles and using the platforms to market their products and services to and interact with potential customers.

News organizations and journalists have also joined social media platforms. They can post breaking news updates, photos,

Before social media platforms emerged, most people got news reports from television, radio, and newspapers.

videos, and other content on social media and reach users worldwide in a few minutes. Social media has given news organizations and journalists rapid access to far greater numbers of people than they have previously had.

The social media platforms do not gather and report news. Rather, they distribute it to users through their networks. The format of social media, built to encourage interaction and engagement, has given ordinary people a way to participate and engage with news organizations and journalists that they did not previously have. Any user can like, share, comment, and discuss stories on social media platforms, which makes it possible for individuals to interact with journalists and with each other. In this way news delivered on social media has become a two-way communication between those who report it and those who read it.

The development of smartphones has enabled social media platforms such as Facebook, Snapchat, TikTok, and Instagram to thrive.

TikTok Misinformation

Misinformation is rampant on social media. According to a 2022 report by researchers at NewsGuard, a journalism and technology tool, when TikTok users search the platform for information on popular news topics such as COVID-19 vaccines or abortion, nearly one-fifth of the video results contain misinformation. The report found that videos containing misinformation often appear in the first five search results, making it more likely they would be viewed by users. This is a concern because of how many people get their news from social media platforms. In 2022, according to a Pew Research Center survey, 10 percent of adults said they used TikTok as a news source, but 26 percent of people under age thirty reported that they regularly get news on the social media platform.

Changing Relationship with News

Even the reporting of news has changed in fundamental ways. Because anyone can create and share content and engage with other users, news reports are no longer limited to traditional news organizations and professional journalists. Anyone with a social media account can become a citizen journalist and post text, photos, and video stories themselves. "Anybody can be an amateur journalist. Now anyone can hop on as an amateur and say, 'This is what you see,'"[7] says Brad Stecklein, a golf instructor in Fort Myers, Florida, who is active on TikTok.

Dozens of amateur journalists posted on social media when Category 4 Hurricane Ian hit Florida in September 2022. Dozens of TikTok users turned to the platform's live stream feature to show real-time video of what was happening on the ground as the hurricane approached. Their live videos showed the storm's torrential rain, howling winds, and rising waters. "I wanted to give an accurate portrayal,"[8] says Stecklein, who live-streamed the storm from his backyard. Thousands of users watched the live videos and sent messages of support.

> "Anybody can be an amateur journalist. Now anyone can hop on as an amateur and say, 'This is what you see.'"[7]
>
> —Brad Stecklein, golf instructor in Fort Myers, Florida, who is active on TikTok

A Twenty-Four-Hour News Cycle

And all of this was happening in real time. Today the public expects news in real time—all day, every day. At any given time, users worldwide are posting, scrolling, and interacting online. When news breaks, journalists no longer have to wait for a newspaper's next printing or a television news program's next airing to inform the public. Instead, they can cover it immediately with a tweet, post, or quick video. Cassandra Garrison, social media and live-news editor at Thomson Reuters, a multinational media corporation, says:

> In the last 10 years, [Twitter] has really taken off as a consistent place for people to turn in urgent situations when they are in need of instant info. This makes it a perfect place for journalists and news orgs to have a space to communicate with their followers. It's also when we see our biggest spikes on Reuters accounts—in times of breaking news when we are fastest with the information.[9]

The ability to report breaking news—as it happens—comes with challenges. Pressure to be the first to report a story has always existed in journalism, but with social media, time for checking sources and information is greatly reduced. Without that extra time, carelessness and mistakes are more likely.

One example of how the rush to report on social media can lead to mistakes happened in February 2021. Trevor Bauer, a pitcher in Major League Baseball (MLB), played for the Cincinnati Reds during the 2020 season, but he became a free agent at the end of the season.

> "In the last 10 years, [Twitter] has really taken off as a consistent place for people to turn in urgent situations when they are in need of instant info. This makes it a perfect place for journalists and news orgs to have a space to communicate with their followers."[9]
>
> —Cassandra Garrison, social media and live-news editor at Thomson Reuters, a multinational media corporation

Social media platforms make it easy to report breaking news, but it's also easy to make mistakes, such as when a reporter erroneously tweeted that Major League Baseball pitcher Trevor Bauer (pictured) had signed to play for the New York Mets instead of the Los Angeles Dodgers.

Bauer was among the best young pitchers in the league and had won the 2020 Cy Young Award, the top individual award for pitchers. Baseball fans were clamoring to know where Bauer would play for the 2021 season. On February 4 Bob Nightengale, a journalist for *USA Today*, tweeted that Bauer had agreed to a new contract with the New York Mets. Minutes later several other baseball reporters tweeted that Nightengale's report was wrong and Bauer had not signed to play for the Mets. The next day Bauer signed with the Los Angeles Dodgers. If Nightengale had taken the time to verify his source, he might not have made this reporting mistake. Nightengale issued an apology a few days later. "Sincerest apologies, particularly to those passionate Mets fans whose hopes were raised, for my erroneous tweet that he had a deal w/ the #Mets. Zero excuses,"[10] Nightengale tweeted.

Building Relationships with the Public

Social media allows journalists to build a public profile and a following that would have been difficult with traditional news reporting. Today most stories online and in conventional outlets include a reporter's Facebook and Twitter usernames as part of his or her byline. Readers who like a journalist's reporting can follow the person on social media to see more of his or her work across news organizations and publications. Journalists can engage with users, share thoughts and opinions about news stories, and debate issues on social media. Social media gives journalists a face to go with their names and lets followers learn about them more personally. These connections can help journalists gain loyal followers.

Becoming more personal is not without risks, however. Users who disagree with or are unhappy with a journalist's reporting can easily reach the journalist and let him or her know their displeasure. In some cases this can cross the line into harassment. Olivia Krupp, a student journalist at the University of Arizona, experienced this harassment firsthand. After writing an article in the school newspaper comparing a student TikTok star to a well-known misogynist, Krupp was targeted and harassed by readers who did not like what she wrote. She received ugly text messages, some of which made rude comments about her appearance. She also received threatening texts, including one that read, "I hope when our society wakes again you are lined up and shot."[11] The calls and messages from hostile readers poured into her phone for days. Her social media accounts filled with hateful comments. On campus, students posted sightings of Krupp on the social platform YikYak. The harassment campaign has made Krupp anxious in public and at school. "Walking to class, it's humiliating to have things like this said about me," she says. "I've had people come up to me when I'm out. I've been getting stares in my classes. It's affected my ability to concentrate and be relaxed in any public setting."[12]

Alternative Social Media Sites

In recent years several new social media platforms have emerged as alternatives to larger, more established sites such as Facebook and Twitter. These alternative platforms, including BitChute, Gab, Gettr, Parler, Ruble, Telegram, and Truth Social, attract a smaller group of news consumers. According to a 2022 Pew Research Center study, most users on these sites say they have found a group of like-minded users, which are frequently Republican and hold conservative views. Those who get news on these alternative sites are mainly satisfied with their news experience, saying they can get information on these sites that they cannot get on other social media platforms, according to the same study. However, critics believe these sites are inaccurate and spread misinformation and bias.

Krupp is not the only journalist who has experienced harassment online. A 2022 Pew Research Center survey noted that 42 percent of journalists said they had experienced job-related harassment or threats at least once in the past year. Most of the harassment occurred online, often on social media. The harassment included threats of physical violence, sexual harassment, racial and ethnic harassment, and exposure of personal information. *Washington Post* columnist Margaret Sullivan has been harassed and threatened on social media, describing it as a very unsettling experience. "Unless you've been there, it's hard to comprehend how deeply destabilizing it is, how it can make you think twice about your next story, or even whether being a journalist is worth it,"[13] she says.

Controlling News Stories

In traditional news outlets, journalists decide what stories to cover and where to place them in newspapers and news programs. Journalists have less control over what stories appear and where they are placed in users' feeds on social media. Instead, a user's network of friends and the social media platform's algorithms influence what news and information users see.

What a person sees in his or her social media feed is influenced by that person's network of friends. An article that is liked and shared multiple times by friends will appear in a person's feed. Instead of an editor deciding what front-page news is, social media friends affect what news articles a user sees. Often, articles with sensational headlines or outrageous claims will get shared repeatedly, making them more likely to be seen on social media even if they are not trustworthy.

Social media algorithms are designed to determine users' interests by analyzing what they have liked, shared, and commented on. The algorithms boost similar content to create a personalized feed for the user. By filling users' feeds with a customized content stream, the social media platforms hope to engage users, generating more advertising money for the platforms. Also, brands can pay to have their content appear in news feeds and catch users' attention. When users see a constant stream of information that agrees with their views, whether from like-minded friends or social media algorithms, they risk forming an echo chamber, where the same perspectives and opinions are constantly repeated while different views are filtered out.

Journalists and news organizations no longer control who creates news content on social media. Anyone can upload content to social media platforms, whether the person has a journalism background or not. And this information rarely goes through the fact-checking or source verification required by traditional news outlets. As a result, false and misleading information can appear in news feeds.

Here to Stay

Social media as a place to get news has been positive in many ways. On social media, more stories can be reported, faster than ever, and distributed to a worldwide audience. Yet the characteristics of social media that benefit news distribution have also created challenges for journalists and users alike.

CHAPTER TWO

False and Misleading Information Goes Viral

The internet and social media have become significant sources of news and information for many people worldwide. People read, watch, or listen to news on social media daily. Often, they take for granted that what they find is accurate and credible, when in fact social media is rife with false information. And when users share false information, often unknowingly, the speed and broad reach of these platforms quickly spread it to millions of other users worldwide.

How False Information Starts

There are many reasons why false information gets mistaken for factual news on social media. Sometimes, journalists rush to tweet or post before all story facts are fully known and understood, which can lead to mistakes. For example, on September 8, 2022, at 3:07 p.m., BBC journalist Yalda Hakim reported on Twitter that Queen Elizabeth II had died. "BREAKING: Queen Elizabeth II has died aged 96. Buckingham Palace has announced."[14] The news sent shock waves across social media. However at the time, the queen was

When a BBC journalist erroneously tweeted on September 8, 2022, that England's Queen Elizabeth II (pictured) had died, that false report sent shock waves across social media. The queen did not die until later that day.

still alive. She died later that day, with the palace announcing her death at 6:30 p.m.

When the BBC confirmed that Hakim's report was wrong, she deleted the tweet and apologized to her followers. "I tweeted that there had been an announcement about the death of the Queen. This was incorrect, there has been no announcement, and so I have deleted the tweet. I apologize,"[15] she wrote. Twitter users criticized Hakim for getting the story wrong. "How can you tweet there has been an announcement when there has been no announcement? Should be ashamed,"[16] said one follower.

Blurring Lines Between Fact and Opinion

At other times, false information spreads on social media because people mistake opinion pieces for factual news. In traditional news reporting, it is much easier to tell the difference between facts that can be proved with objective evidence and opinions that are based on beliefs or values. Newspapers, television, and radio news programs typically use labels such as "editorial," "op-ed," "commentary," or "analysis" to distinguish opinion pieces from factual news reports. Some online news sites do the same.

Clear labels like these are rarely used on social media, where the line between fact and opinion is often blurred. Anyone with an internet connection can create and post content on social media. Users frequently have little information about the content creators, including the source of their stories and whether they have checked their facts. Plus, social media platforms do not require content creators to disclose whether their content is fact or opinion. Users are left to figure out the difference on their own. "News consumers today are confronted with a tangle of statements and assertions that run the gamut from purely factual to purely opinion. Being able to quickly tell where a news statement fits on that spectrum is key to being an informed reader or viewer,"[17] says Amy Mitchell, director of journalism research at the Pew Research Center.

Accuracy Prompt

A simple reminder to think about accuracy may slow the spread of misinformation on social media. In 2021 researchers at the University of Regina in Canada conducted a study on Twitter and sent a simple accuracy prompt to more than five thousand users who had recently shared news links from Breitbart or Infowars, two websites known for publishing biased content and conspiracy theories. The prompt was a seemingly random question from another Twitter account that asked people for their opinion about the accuracy of one nonpolitical news headline. The goal was not to get a response but to remind people about the idea of accuracy. For the next twenty-four hours, researchers tracked how often the people shared links from sites of high-quality information and from sites known for low-quality information. (The study relied on professional fact-checkers to determine the quality of a site's information.) On average, the people shared more higher-quality information after being reminded to think about accuracy than they did before. The researchers believe that simple reminders about accuracy can have a noticeable effect on users' sharing behavior on social media, which in turn could slow the spread of misinformation.

Making it even more difficult to distinguish between fact and opinion is the way social media feeds organize content. Fact-based news reports appear next to vacation photos, opinion pieces, and funny memes. The news feeds format each type of content similarly, so there is no easy way to spot the difference at first glance. "When getting their news these days, Americans need to quickly decide how to understand news-related statements that can come in snippets or with little or no context,"[18] says Mitchell.

As a result, social media users often have trouble distinguishing factual reports from opinionated content. A 2018 Pew Research Center study proved precisely that. In the study, researchers created five factual statements and five opinion statements. They asked five thousand adult participants to identify each type of statement. Only 35 percent correctly identified all five opinion statements. Even fewer, 26 percent, correctly identified all five factual statements. Most participants confused the two types of

The way that social media platforms organize material makes it difficult for users to distinguish between factual reports and opinion-only content.

statements, thinking the opinions were fact and vice versa. "One especially salient finding is that the basic task of differentiating between factual and opinion news statements presents somewhat of a challenge to Americans," says Mitchell. "For us, this raises questions about how well the public is equipped to parse through news in the current environment."[19]

Paula Schuck, a Canadian journalist and mother of two teens, sees firsthand how teens have difficulty telling the difference between fact-based news and other content, such as opinions or ads on social media. She says:

> "They wake up to TikTok, spend breakfast on Snapchat and DM friends privately all day long on Instagram and Discord. Ads and news pop up constantly on all of the channels. Their news gathering is so very different than mine was at that age and it's 24/7 in the palm of your hand."[20]
>
> —Paula Schuck, journalist and mother of two teens

They wake up to TikTok, spend breakfast on Snapchat and DM friends privately all day long on Instagram and Discord. Ads and news pop up constantly on all of the channels. Their news gathering is so very different than mine was at that age and it's 24/7 in the palm of your hand. If the *Daily Mail* sponsors an ad on Snapchat that's labeled as news, one of them frequently believes that as fact. . . . I see them gathering their news frequently via TikTok and Snapchat. Often that's simply some TikTok friend spouting off about their opinion of Trump or Biden, or Trudeau. That is not news, nor is it reliable, but too often they take it as such.[20]

Information Overload

The difficulty of recognizing the difference between fact and opinion can be partly explained by the sheer volume of content that flows through social media. To avoid being bogged down with so many stories, most people scroll quickly through their feeds and react even more quickly. Often, they share, comment, or like content before taking the time to think critically about what they find.

Research supports the idea that information overload distracts users and contributes to sharing misinformation on social media. A 2021 study by researchers at the University of Regina in Canada concluded that the format of social media and all of the competing content found there creates a distraction for users. Distracted users are more likely to share false information even when that is not their intention. Researchers David Rand and Gordon Pennycock say, "People fall for fake news when they rely on their intuitions and emotions, and therefore don't think enough about what they are reading—a problem that is likely exacerbated on social media, where people scroll quickly, are distracted by a deluge of information, and encounter news mixed in with emotionally engaging baby photos, cat videos and the like."[21]

During the COVID-19 pandemic, a lot of false and misleading information was spread intentionally on social media. However, many users shared stories they believed to be true. Mixed in with

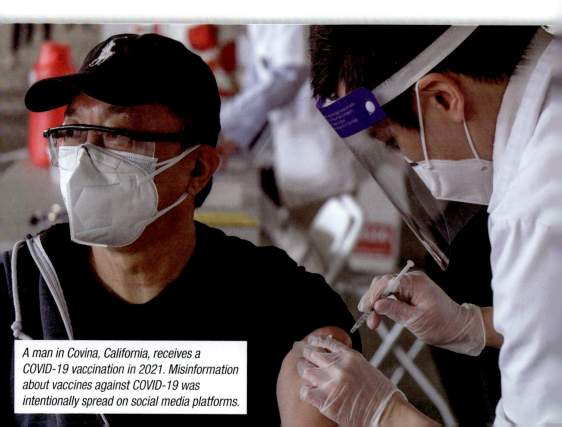

A man in Covina, California, receives a COVID-19 vaccination in 2021. Misinformation about vaccines against COVID-19 was intentionally spread on social media platforms.

factual stories about the origins of the virus, treatments, and vaccines were many others that were either misleading or completely untrue. For example, in January 2020 conspiracy theorist David Zublick uploaded a video to his YouTube channel that reported that the coronavirus that caused COVID-19 was a manufactured bioweapon designed to control the world's population. His 160,000 subscribers watched the video. Many then shared it with others who believed it to be true.

> "If I've learned anything . . . it's that the potential to spread information rapidly really exists through social media platforms."[22]
>
> —Abdu Sharkawy, infectious diseases specialist at University Health Network

Misinformation about treatments also circulated widely on social media. In 2020 a post that spread on Facebook and Twitter told people that garlic could cure COVID-19 and suggested that users boil eight garlic cloves in water to make a soup. Although Facebook labeled the claim "factually inaccurate," many still believed it was true. Other stories about purported treatments such as chlorine dioxide, vitamins, and nasal sprays also spread via social media. "If I've learned anything . . . it's that the potential to spread information rapidly really exists through social media platforms," Abdu Sharkawy, an infectious diseases specialist at University Health Network, said at the time. "But some people with little background in science or health care have anointed themselves as experts and give people advice. It's very damaging and hasn't helped at all."[22]

In some cases rapidly spreading COVID-19 misinformation about masks, vaccines, and treatments cost lives. Brian Lee Hitchens from Jupiter, Florida, experienced this firsthand. When the pandemic began in 2020, he and his wife, Erin, read many supposed news accounts on Facebook that convinced them that the virus was not real. "We thought the government was using it to distract us or it was to do with 5G [cell towers]. So we didn't follow the rules or seek help sooner," says Brian. Because they believed what they read on social media, the couple did not take recommended precautions such as wearing masks or limiting social contact. Then

Consequences of False Information

The spread of false information on social media can have serious consequences. In a nationwide 2022 poll by the University of Chicago Pearson Institute/AP-NORC, 91 percent of American adults agreed that misinformation is a growing problem. Respondents said they believe misinformation fuels extreme political views and hate crimes based on gender, race, or religion. Many people also believe that the spread of false information is harming American democracy by increasing public distrust in the government, creating doubt around elections and disrupting the democratic process.

in May 2020, when Brian and his wife both contracted COVID-19, they resisted getting medical help. When their illness worsened, both had to be hospitalized. Erin's condition became critical. She was sedated and placed on a ventilator. While Brian eventually recovered, his wife did not. Erin died in August 2020 at age forty-six from complications linked to COVID-19. "And now I realize that coronavirus is definitely not fake. It's out there, and it's spreading,"[23] Brian said shortly before his wife died.

Disinformation

The qualities that enable the rapid spread of misinformation on social media also make it easy to spread disinformation. Disinformation campaigns are meant to stir up chaos and confusion, spread propaganda, and create political instability. They are often orchestrated by authoritarian governments or other political entities. This was evident in a May 2020 disinformation campaign that targeted the Qatar government. On May 4, 2020, an anonymous Twitter account tweeted that there had been an explosion outside the country's capital city of Doha. Soon after, another account replied to the tweet and falsely claimed there had been a coup attempt against Qatar's emir, Sheikh Tamim bin Hamad Al Thani. Soon hashtags like #coupinQatar began to trend on Twitter. Within hours, hundreds of thousands of tweets circulated about the alleged coup, and it became the number one trending Twitter topic in Qatar and

Saudi Arabia. Tweets reported that Qatar's former prime minister, Hamad bin Jassim, was trying to overthrow the emir.

The problem with these tweets is that there had been no coup attempt. The widely shared reports were revealed to be a ruse designed to discredit the Qatari government and make it appear unstable. "It is clear that the rumors about an alleged coup attempt in Qatar did not organically materialize on social media but were the product of a coordinated campaign,"[24] Marc Owen Jones, assistant professor of Middle East studies and digital humanities at Qatar's Hamad bin Khalifa University, explained at the time.

Once the coup claim was proved false, Twitter suspended many of the accounts that contributed to the disinformation campaign. But by then the damage had been done. Independent news outlets worldwide had picked up the story and published reports of a rumored coup in Qatar—without bothering to verify whether the rumors were true. Jones says:

> Disinformation campaigns often seek not to prove the claims they make, but to provoke discord, instability, and uncertainty in their targets. Simply by reporting that there were "rumors of a coup in Qatar," therefore, many independent media outlets played into the hands of the propagandists behind this campaign. The real story is not that there were rumors of a coup, but that there was a disinformation campaign designed to give the illusion of a coup. In an age where disinformation is rife, even a technically factual report on social media trends can fan the flame of fake news.[25]

What Is the Truth?

Social media sites allow people to quickly find news and information anywhere and anytime. However, the ease with which news and information can appear on social media has created challenges for many users, who must learn how to distinguish what is factual versus what is not.

CHAPTER THREE

Social Media Creates Echo Chambers

One of the unique features of social media is its ability to curate specific content for individual users. Social media algorithms take data such as likes, shares, comments, and searches to determine what a person is interested in seeing online. Then these algorithms promote content that matches what a person wants to see and encourages engagement on the platform. The strategy is a winning one for social media companies. The higher user engagement rises, the more likely it is that advertisers will buy valuable ad space on these platforms—and use the algorithms to place the ads in front of the users most likely to respond.

However, there is an unintended consequence of creating tailored social media feeds that feel comfortable and familiar. It also creates echo chambers in which people increasingly see only content with similar viewpoints and perspectives because that is what the algorithms promote. At the same time, the algorithms push content that does not agree with a person's interests and views lower in their feed, so they are less likely to see it. As a result, users miss out on a wide range of ideas and topics, creating a biased media experience.

Echo Chambers

Information and news come from many sources and represent many viewpoints. But when people are repeatedly exposed only to information, perspectives, and opinions that reflect what they already know or believe, they may have trouble even considering other facts or views. This is often described as an echo chamber. Echo chambers reinforce a person's existing views by limiting the scope of what that person reads or hears on any given topic.

Echo chambers are supported by confirmation bias, a type of bias in which a person tends to pay attention to and favor information that confirms what they already believe. Confirmation bias is a universal human trait; everyone has some of it. On social media, confirmation bias can funnel users into groups where most people think the same way and hold similar beliefs. "Social media sites foster confirmation bias because of their basic function. Regardless of the specific algorithm, social media sites like Facebook, Reddit, Twitter, Instagram, and even YouTube, serve the same basic function: to connect groups of like-minded users

Social media algorithms use data such as likes, shares, and comments to determine what individual users are interested in seeing online.

> "The fact that social media platforms confirm what we already believe is the reason many people use them in the first place. If the platforms didn't do that, they wouldn't be successful."[27]
>
> —David McRaney, *Science* journalist

together based on shared content preferences,"[26] says Marielle DeVos, an American University student in political science.

Confirmation bias may even explain why people are drawn to social media. "The fact that social media platforms confirm what we already believe is the reason many people use them in the first place. If the platforms didn't do that, they wouldn't be successful,"[27] says *Science* journalist David McRaney.

Many people experienced echo chambers during the COVID-19 pandemic. Perhaps they did not know anyone who had died of COVID-19. Perhaps they had a long-standing distrust of government, so when a friend posted an article on Facebook about pharmaceutical companies conspiring with politicians to create the COVID-19 scare to control people, this article rang true. Then these people began searching social media to learn more and turned up articles that described COVID-19 as noth-

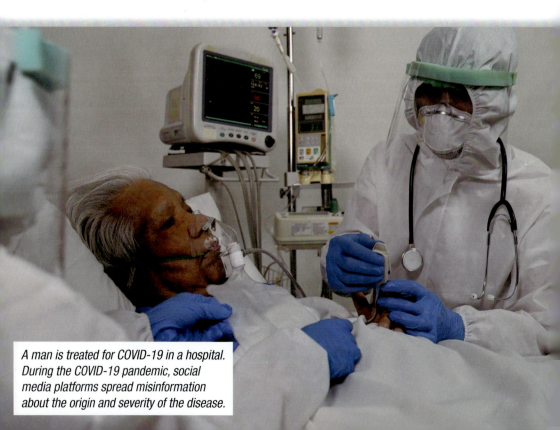

A man is treated for COVID-19 in a hospital. During the COVID-19 pandemic, social media platforms spread misinformation about the origin and severity of the disease.

The Exposure Effect

Social media promotes another type of bias called the exposure effect. Exposure effect is the idea that when a person is repeatedly exposed to the same news or information from many sources, that person is more likely to believe and reshare it. While this bias is part of human nature, social media makes it easier for people to be bombarded with the same information from many sources. When information goes viral on social media and is shared over and over by many users, the exposure effect causes users to pay more attention to it. They believe that if everyone is sharing information, it must be important. Social media platforms like Facebook, Twitter, YouTube, and Instagram often place popular content prominently in users' feeds, along with how many views, likes, and shares it has gotten. However, just because something is popular does not mean it is accurate or even newsworthy.

ing more than the flu. They may have joined a new social media group in which they encountered other people who expressed similar suspicions about the dangers of COVID-19.

Echo chambers are not unique to social media. They exist anywhere people get information, whether online or offline. However, the internet and social media make it easier for echo chambers to thrive because the whole point of social media is to provide an easy way to connect with like-minded people, groups, and news sources.

Filter Bubbles

Social media platforms and the algorithms they use to present personalized feeds create a type of echo chamber called a filter bubble. The term *filter bubble* refers to the way social media and internet search engines filter information before it reaches a user. Anywhere a person goes online, algorithms behind the scenes track the websites they visit and what they click on. For example, a user might search for information about skis. Suddenly, multiple advertisements and content about skiing, ski equipment, and ski vacations pop up on the person's social media feeds. The algorithms used by websites and social media platforms to track his or her online activity now show content these algorithms predict the user will want to see. This process also creates filter bubbles by promoting information and content that already matches a person's likes and perspectives.

Some social media platforms are more likely than others to create filter bubbles. In a 2021 study, researchers from the Sapienza University of Rome in Italy found that users on Facebook and Twitter were more likely to segregate into filter bubbles. In the study, researchers analyzed four platforms—Facebook, Twitter, Reddit, and Gab—and explored the key differences between the platforms and how those differences influenced the formation of filter bubbles. Researchers analyzed more than 100 million pieces of content on controversial subjects such as gun control, vaccination, and abortion. They found that users were more likely to segregate into filter bubbles on platforms that used algorithms to push personalized content to users. Also, segregation was stronger on platforms like Facebook and Twitter, which give users less control over their feeds. For example, on Facebook, users cannot adjust their feeds to see a simple chronological list of content shared by their network. Reddit, which relies less on algorithms and allows users more input on what they see, was less likely to segregate users into filter bubbles. Walter Quattrociocchi, one of the lead researchers and a computer science professor at Sapienza University of Rome, says:

> While looking at our data, we found differences in levels of segregation. The highest was found on Facebook and Twitter. Moreover, we also found a clear difference between sites where users could tweak their feed to edit the types and amounts of posts they saw—more tweaking tended to mean less segregation. Facebook, notably, does not have such an option, while Reddit's tweaking options are very strong. Hence, higher segregation was found on Facebook than on Reddit.[28]

Becoming More Extreme

Social media's echo chambers segregate users into like-minded groups that reinforce existing bias. They may also help shift the group to more extreme political beliefs. As users become isolated from opposing political views within their bubble, a sense of "us versus them" can grow. Conservative users surround themselves with conservative content, while liberal users are surrounded by liberal content. When each side is confronted with opposing views, they interpret them to fit their own perspective instead of trying to understand these other views. Over time, their political views can move further away from center and toward either extreme. A study published in March 2020 supported the idea that social media increases extreme political beliefs. In the study, researchers conducted an experiment in which participants stayed off Facebook for a month. Then they answered questions about their political views. The researchers found that staying away from Facebook significantly reduced the subjects' polarization on policy issues. "That's consistent with the view that people are seeing political content on social media that does tend to make them more upset, more angry at the other side [and more likely] to have stronger views on specific issues," says Matthew Gentzkow, a Stanford University economist and study coauthor.

Quoted in Paul Barrett et al., "How Tech Platforms Fuel U.S. Political Polarization and What Government Can Do About It," *Techtank* (blog), Brookings Institution, September 27, 2021. www.brookings.edu.

Once a user encounters a filter bubble on social media, the platform's basic structure encourages users to create networks of like-minded people. As a result, people tend to self-segregate into groups with similar backgrounds, opinions, and perspectives. Filter bubbles make it easier for social media echo chambers to grow.

Why Are Social Media's Echo Chambers a Problem?

Social media's echo chambers become problematic when more people turn to these platforms to get their news. Social media's algorithms push stories and sources that users already agree with and limit stories that do not fit these parameters. This means that users may miss out on information and news stories from a variety of sources and perspectives. A barrier forms that makes it more difficult for users to find new ideas and perspectives. And many users do not even realize that this is happening. Website and social media algorithms operate behind the scenes. Because those actions are largely invisible to users, most people have no way of knowing what selections are being made and what else might be available.

For users unknowingly stuck in an echo chamber, the problem gets worse. Users might think they are getting the complete story based on the news content they read online, but in reality, they only see part of the story. It is more difficult to discuss the facts and make an informed judgment with incomplete information. When they are armed with half the facts, users are less likely to understand the full scope of a story and are often unwilling to consider information and viewpoints that contradict what they already believe.

Another key characteristic of social media—the ability for anyone to upload content—also becomes a bigger problem in echo chambers. In traditional news outlets, journalists and news organizations act as gatekeepers to decide what news and information get published. Professional journalists evaluate content for accuracy, use credible sources, and determine what is newsworthy. However, on social media anyone can create and upload content. When a social media algorithm picks up this content and promotes it to specific groups of users, there is little vetting of sources or accuracy.

Increasing Polarization and Division

Social media promotes news and information that matches what users already believe, no matter how extreme. And the platforms do little to make sure that information is accurate. Their algorithms also screen out opposing information that might change a person's mind, give him or her a new perspective, or inform the other side of a story. These conditions make social media and its echo chambers fertile soil for division and polarization to grow. "There's little doubt in my mind that the way our media ecosystem works is enflaming political sectarianism. Social media is not focused on making the world a better place; it's primarily focused on engagement, so it listens to us and gives us what we want," says Eli Finkel, a psychology professor at Northwestern University who has researched political polarization."[29]

> "There's little doubt in my mind that the way our media ecosystem works is enflaming political sectarianism. Social media is not focused on making the world a better place; it's primarily focused on engagement, so it listens to us and gives us what we want."[29]
>
> —Eli Finkel, psychology professor at Northwestern University

Journalist Max Fisher has studied social media's impact on daily life and believes the platforms contribute to increasing polarization in today's society. He explains that many people do not realize the polarizing, one-sided view social media presents. "When you log on to Facebook, Twitter, or YouTube, you think that what you are seeing is a neutral reflection of your community, and what [your community] is talking about,"[30] he says.

Social media platforms promote content that will increase user engagement, contributing to polarization in today's society.

Instead, platforms are trying to promote content that will increase user engagement. And they have learned that outrageous posts that trigger strong emotions are the best way to do that. Fisher says:

> In fact, what you were seeing, and what you were experiencing, are choices made by these incredibly sophisticated automated systems that are designed to figure out exactly what combination of posts, what way to sequence those posts, how to present them to you will most engage certain very specific cognitive triggers and cognitive weak points that are meant to get certain emotions going. They are meant to trigger certain impulses and instincts that will make you feel really compelled to come back to the platform to spend a lot of time on it.[31]

Half the Story

Social media makes it easier to get news and information. At first, it may sound like a good idea for social media platforms to personalize users' online experiences. With so much content online, having a way to filter it and show what is most important and interesting is attractive to many. However, these same algorithms and like-minded friend groups can make it more difficult for users to get all the information they need. If they are not careful, users might find they are only getting half the story on social media instead of all the facts.

CHAPTER FOUR

Evaluating News Sources

Stories in the news can inform and inspire people to make more educated decisions and have a greater understanding of the world around them. However, social media platforms have changed how news is created, distributed, and consumed. Anyone can create news content and post it on social media. From there, users engage with stories that resonate with them and share these stories on their social networks. As a result, news spreads faster and farther than ever on social media networks.

Yet social media was initially designed as an entertainment and social venue where users could connect with family, friends, and other like-minded people, not as a place to find news. The characteristics that make social media platforms a great place for social connections—like the ability for anyone to create content and the algorithms used to curate content for users based on their interests—can pose problems for distributing news.

Challenges for Social Media Users

In social media, traditional journalistic and publishing standards are not always followed. Anyone with an internet-connected device can create and publish social media content. That content may be fact, opinion, or even false. Content ranges from personal blogs to sponsored ads

> "Many assume that because young people are fluent in social media, they are equally savvy about what they find there. Our work shows the opposite."[32]
>
> —Sam Wineburg, researcher from Stanford University

to scientific research data. Social media content can be published by professional journalists and news organizations that use fact-checkers and verify sources or created by a high school student obsessed with conspiracy theories.

The freedom for anyone to become a creator on social media means that users need to learn how to evaluate what they encounter on these platforms and determine its reliability. It is a task that many find challenging. Even young people who have grown up with social media find it difficult to differentiate verified news from other types of content. In a 2020 study, researchers from Stanford University tested how well students could evaluate what they saw on social media. They found that middle school students could not distinguish between reported news and sponsored content. High school students relied on an unverified photo as proof a story was true, and college students could not detect bias in tweets. "Many assume that because young people are fluent in social media, they are equally savvy about what they find there. Our work shows the opposite,"[32] says Sam Wineburg, one of the study's authors.

Researchers say that although young people readily use social media, they are not necessarily good at distinguishing between verified news and other types of content.

Media Literacy

As more people turn to social media for news, media literacy becomes an increasingly important skill set to acquire. Media literacy, as defined by the National Association for Media Literacy Education, is "the ability to access, analyze, evaluate, create, and act using all forms of communication."[33] Media literacy gives people the ability to understand and evaluate the messages they receive from media and create and share their own messages. Mary Kate Lonergan, a media literacy educator, says:

> Think of all the things you read in a day—emails, books, and the news. What about Facebook posts, Instagram captions, Tweets, editorials, ads, and subtitles? How about maps, memes, and infographics? Do you read each in the same way? You likely employ a certain set of skills and strategies when you engage with each piece of media. But given the new and ever-changing ways we use technology to receive and communicate information, to be literate in today's constantly connected world involves skills beyond simply reading and writing in the traditional sense.[34]

While media literacy is as relevant offline as it is online, these skills become critical when dealing with news and information that flows over social media. "Being media literate empowers students to ask questions, make sound judgments rooted in fact and evidence,"[35] says Lonergan.

One of the essential media literacy skills is evaluating and identifying credible news sources. When getting news on social media, users must be able to assess information and determine how accurate it is, how reliable it is, and whether it has any bias.

> "Given the new and ever-changing ways we use technology to receive and communicate information, to be literate in today's constantly connected world involves skills beyond simply reading and writing in the traditional sense."[34]
>
> —Mary Kate Lonergan, media literacy educator

> "With students and adults alike, it's just easy to look at stuff on social media and take it as it is and not question it. It can be difficult to push through that apathy, but it's well worth trying."[36]
>
> —Paul Blakesley, teacher of media and information literacy at Palmer High School in Colorado

Because misinformation, disinformation, and biased content circulate widely across social media platforms, identifying trustworthy sources has become more important than ever. "With students and adults alike, it's just easy to look at stuff on social media and take it as it is and not question it," says Paul Blakesley, who teaches media and information literacy at Palmer High School in Colorado Springs, Colorado. "It can be difficult to push through that apathy, but it's well worth trying,"[36] he adds.

Evaluate Sources

Consider the source is a common theme in any discussion of media literacy. But how, exactly, does a person go about doing that? Gabrielle Casieri, a library media specialist at Lawrence Intermediate School in New Jersey, suggests the types of questions to ask yourself when reading news on social media—or getting news from any source, for that matter. "Students need to start considering from the time they can read, 'Who is giving me this information? What are their qualifications? Are they an expert?' They need to consider all of the aspects of a source, and right now, we just don't do that,"[37] Casieri says.

When evaluating a source, users should not mistake celebrity for expertise. Anyone can make a statement online about any subject. The question to consider is whether that person has expertise or particular knowledge about the subject matter on which they are commenting. A famous actor or musician might be considered an expert or at least knowledgeable about his or her craft and thus something of an authority on that topic. But an actor or musician who posts information about the safety or risks of vaccines is not an authority on that topic and should not be viewed as such. Instead, a scientist with a background in immunology or a public health physician would be a more reliable source on this topic.

Finding a Credible Source

Finding a credible source can be challenging on social media. Credible sources aim to teach or inform readers and do not have a hidden agenda. Some of the most credible sources are scholarly articles or pieces written by educational organizations. When trying to determine whether a source is credible, here are a few steps to follow:

- Check the author's credentials and background. See whether he or she has the expertise or experience to write about the subject.
- Check whether the author cites any additional sources.
- Look to see whether the source was created by a reputable publisher.
- Check the date of the source and make sure it is current.
- Look at the source's website and see whether there are any relevant links for readers.
- Check for any reviews or endorsements of the source.

Understanding Misinformation and Disinformation

Content on social media takes many different forms. Some content can lead to confusion. The type of content that sometimes brings confusion is satire. Through the use of humor, exaggeration, irony, parody, and metaphor, satire pointedly pokes fun at people, organizations, and institutions. Politics and culture are frequent targets of satire. Although the aim of satire is to make fun of its subject, it is also intended to make a point. Sometimes, though, people misunderstand what they're reading and mistake satire for actual news.

The likelihood of this happening is heightened by the workings of social media. If a person goes directly to a website that is well known for publishing satire, there's little chance of confusion. But when an article shows up in social media news feeds with hundreds of other articles, many readers will not recognize that article as satire.

Communication researchers at the Conversation, a nonprofit online news organization, set out to study satire, misinformation,

Researchers have found that many people are fooled by articles on satirical online publications, like the Onion.

and social media in 2019. For six months, they looked at the most shared fake political stories on social media, including satire. Then they asked a representative group of Americans whether they believed the stories and how confident they were in their assessment. The surveys included satire from both the Babylon Bee and the Onion, well-known satirical sites.

Researchers found that many people were fooled by the satirical articles, although their political affiliation affected which articles they believed. Of the twenty-three satiric articles from the Babylon Bee, at least 15 percent of Republican respondents expressed confidence that eight of the articles were true. For example, The Bee ran an article that focused on Vermont Senator Bernie Sanders, who has long championed wiping out all student loan debt. In this story, Sanders was characterized as being critical of a billionaire who paid off student debt for graduates of Morehouse College, a historically black college and/or university (HBCU). The suggestion is that Sanders did not support student debt relief, which is untrue. Satire from the Onion also fooled respondents.

Nearly one in eight Democrats found believable a story claiming that Trump White House counselor Kellyanne Conway questioned the value of the rule of law. The suggestion is that Conway, as a member of Trump's inner circle, believed that U.S. laws did not apply to her, which is untrue. Scott Dikkers, the founding editor of the Onion, says readers need to be more aware of the content they read online. "This whole situation should send us all a message . . . like a laser beam right to our brains, a clear and powerful message that is so powerful, it can make us more critical thinkers. . . . That message is simply—don't believe everything you read,"[38] he says. To recognize satire, users can investigate the article's source. Sites that publish satire often have disclaimers or descriptions noting their role as a publisher of satirical material.

Some content found on social media leads to confusion because it contains selected facts that support the author's point of view and leaves out facts that paint a full or more accurate picture. While the information provided may be accurate, without the added facts, the story may be misleading. In a 2020 survey by the Pew Research Center, two-thirds of US adults said that the news sources they turned to most often presented facts that favored one side of an issue in 2020 election coverage. When these incomplete stories end up on social media, the one-sided information they present can cause more confusion.

Clickbait articles are another example of misleading content that uses shocking headlines to entice users to click on them. Every click drives traffic to the creator's website and generates income for the website owners. Often the entire piece does not match the headline, and sometimes may even be about an entirely different subject. When users scrolling through social media feeds just read these shocking headlines without verifying the supporting information, they can be tricked into believing outlandish claims are actual news.

Some content found on social media is deliberately false. Usually this type of article, a form of disinformation, is meant to create public chaos and confusion, generate profits, or influence political

Fact-Checking

One way to combat false information on social media is by fact-checking information found in news content. Several websites have been established to help readers check the facts in news they find online and offline. FactCheck.org is a nonpartisan, nonprofit website established by the Annenberg Public Policy Center to help the public find the truth. The site evaluates the accuracy of information found in news releases, television ads, debates, speeches, interviews, and more. In 2023 the site evaluated the accuracy of President Joe Biden's State of the Union address. In one fact-checking example, the website stated, "Biden said he has cut the deficit by a record $1.7 trillion, but most of that was due to expiring emergency pandemic spending." Another fact-checking website is PolitiFact, which provides independent fact-checking on a range of issues in the news. The site fact-checked the Republican response to the 2023 State of the Union address, given by Arkansas governor Sarah Huckabee Sanders. In one example, Sanders claimed that "the Biden administration refuses to secure the border." PolitiFact stated, "This ignores enforcement by border authorities, including surveillance technology. Border security funding under Biden is comparable to funding under Trump's administration."

FactCheck.org, "Fact-Checking the State of the Union," February 8, 2023. www.factcheck.org.

Quoted in PolitiFact, "Fact-Checking Sarah Huckabee Sanders' Republican Response to Joe Biden's 2023 State of the Union," February 8, 2023. www.politifact.com.

action or reactions. The content can be completely false, or it can contain text, audio, video, or images that have been manipulated. Sometimes, governments may produce disinformation to control their citizens or make their leaders appear more powerful.

Reading Laterally to Verify Content

For years, literacy experts have taught students to cross-check facts and information within an article or website to verify it. But now with all sorts of misinformation and misleading content appearing on social media, experts have found that a different strategy called lateral reading can be more effective at evaluating sources and verifying information on social media.

In lateral reading, users verify information by looking outside a website or article. They perform web searches and open multiple browser tabs to verify facts and check sources. They cross-check information across many sites and sources to verify its trustworthiness. Lateral reading can help users determine whether information has been verified by other sources and gather information about a source's reputation. "People often assume that social media posts with higher levels of engagement—more likes, shares and comments—or that come from accounts with lots of followers and engagement are more reliable. Again, that's not true; the best way to decide is to read laterally about the source or investigate the claims a post makes through sources you trust,"[39] says Sarah McGrew, an assistant professor at the University of Maryland's College of Education.

In a 2022 study, researchers at Stanford University found that students who learned lateral reading strategies significantly improved their ability to identify unreliable online information by 71 percent. McGrew says:

> We should train ourselves to think about where the information we see is coming from and whether we trust that source. . . . Anytime you see a site or a post whose source you don't recognize, open a new tab and search outside the site for more information about its source. If you leave the site and do a quick search for more information, you'll likely learn so much more about the author or organization than what you'd find on the "About Us" page or profile.[40]

At Christ Church Episcopal School in Greenville, South Carolina, teachers like Jamie Gregory are helping students develop lateral reading skills to evaluate news they see on social media. In one exercise, students were given an Instagram story with the headline "Head of Pfizer Research: Covid Vaccine Is Female Sterilization." The article came from an unverified source and was published in 2020, just as the United States was rolling out the first COVID-19 vaccines. Gregory instructed students in her journalism class to analyze the article. Using lessons they learned about lateral reading, the students realized the best way to analyze the article was to verify it by searching other sources. Students quickly found other news stories and academic studies that refuted the sterilization claim and discredited the former Pfizer scientist at its center. They learned that research never confirmed claims that the COVID-19 vaccine caused fertility problems in men or women. "They really had to do the work to figure it out for themselves. It felt important that they had developed this skill. And it does make me feel hopeful going forward,"[41] says Gregory.

Read Deep and Confirm the Details

Too often, people on social media read a flashy news headline and quickly hit "share" to pass it on to their network. Being media literate on social media means taking a moment to pause and confirm details about a story before taking it as truth. In addition to evaluating the story's source and reading laterally, users can read beyond the headline and confirm a story's details to ensure that it is what it claims to be.

First, check the date of the story. Often, people on social media recycle old stories with new, outrageous headlines. The story may sound familiar, but it is hard to remember in a social media world flooded with news whether one has seen it before. Sometimes, those spreading it do not care if it is old news, because it matches their views. That's what happened in 2019 when a CBS News article titled "U.S. Votes Against Anti-Nazi Resolution at U.N." spread on Facebook. Many people who shared the article commented that it was another example of President Donald Trump refusing to condemn Nazis. Those who already did not like Trump were eager to share an article that appeared to be unflattering to him. Yet a simple date check shows that the story was initially written in 2016 when President Barack Obama was in office. The US opposed the resolution because officials believed the

When an article implying that President Donald Trump (pictured) refused to condemn Nazis spread on Facebook, users who disliked Trump were inclined to believe it.

wording was too restrictive of the fundamental right of freedom of expression. Old stories may no longer be relevant or may contain outdated facts.

Users should also think about what purpose the content serves. Credible news content aims to inform users. Yet on social media, users often find articles and content purposely designed to spark an emotional response. Articles written to stir anger, outrage, fear, or other emotions may be less reliable sources of information and often contain inaccurate information or bias.

False, misleading, or out-of-context photos can also confuse or deceive users on social media. Sometimes, older images are authentic but are used out of context as evidence of unrelated, recent events. For example, Turning Point USA, a conservative group with more than 1.5 million Facebook followers, posted a photo in February 2019 that showed empty grocery store shelves. The group captioned the photo, "YUP! #SocialismSucks." However, the image of the empty shelves was not related to socialism at all. Instead, it was taken in 2011 in Japan after a large earthquake. To protect against this type of misinformation, users can do a reverse image search to learn where a photo has been used previously and confirm its accuracy.

Learning to Navigate News on Social Media

Even though many people admit they do not trust social media as a news source, that role is unlikely to change. Social media has become such an integral part of daily life that people will still use it despite their doubts. Concerns about fake news and other biased content on social media have done little to stop billions of users worldwide from checking their favorite platforms daily—for messages, news, and other content. As a result, it becomes essential that users understand how to navigate the news on these platforms so they can become well-informed participants.

CHAPTER FIVE

Recognizing Bias

All journalists—like people everywhere—have biases. But some journalists, and some media outlets, make no attempt to recognize and manage their biases. So it is up to news consumers to do that. Recognizing biased news accounts can be difficult, especially when people get all their news on social media. Social media's algorithms push content that matches user interests and views and encourages users to connect with like-minded people. When everyone is repeating the same information and views on social media, it becomes more difficult to recognize bias in all of its forms.

What Is Media Bias?

In general, bias is the tendency to show favor toward or against someone or something. Often, bias is influenced by a person's background, culture, and personal experiences. Bias can cause a person to stereotype other people or groups. For example, a teacher with a bias that girls are better than boys at writing might always pick a girl to be the school newspaper editor. Sometimes, a person is aware of their personal bias, called explicit bias. But at other times, a person may not be aware he or she is biased, which is called implicit or unconscious bias. "Until we become aware of our biases, and how these attitudes and opinions emerge through the language we use, we can fall into what's known

Media bias can affect the stories that journalists choose to cover, resulting in incomplete, misleading, and skewed news reporting.

as the bias confirmation trap—we see opinion with which we agree as fact and information with which we disagree as false,"[42] says Jacquelyn Whiting, a high school library media specialist.

Like all people, journalists and the news organizations they work for have some level of bias, both explicit and unconscious.

"Bias is a part of any source of information; the issue is the degree of transparency. When a text is laden with super-charged words and images, the bias is obvious. When the language is more subtle, we are more inclined to miss it,"[43] says Whiting.

Media bias can affect the stories journalists and news organizations choose to cover. It can impact the level of attention given a story as

> "Until we become aware of our biases, and how these attitudes and opinions emerge through the language we use, we can fall into what's known as the bias confirmation trap—we see opinion with which we agree as fact and information with which we disagree as false."[42]
>
> —Jacquelyn Whiting, high school library media specialist

well as the perspective and language used to tell that story. Media bias can lean left, favoring liberal viewpoints, or lean right, favoring conservative viewpoints. Media bias can also show favor toward the perspective of government, business, and organizations. No matter which way bias leans, media bias can result in inaccurate, incomplete, misleading, and skewed news reporting.

Many times, journalists and news organizations are unaware of their bias. Their unconscious bias may occur because they lack access to all the facts needed to present a balanced report. However, the media also regularly publishes stories with explicit bias. In these stories, journalists use their platform to paint an image of an event, group, or person that matches their personal beliefs or the views of the news outlet they work for.

How Media Bias Appears

Media bias, both explicit and unconscious, appears in many ways. Sometimes, media bias is ideological. A journalist or news organization might want to influence the views of their readers, viewers,

Checking for Bias

Readers who are trying to determine whether a source or article is biased can check a news resource online. AllSides is an online site that evaluates the political bias of media reports. The website rates over eight hundred news sources on a five-point scale and gives ratings of left, leans left, center, leans right, and right. It also presents different versions of similar news stories from different perspectives to help readers step outside of a filter bubble and see all sides of an issue or event. For example, when President Joe Biden made a surprise trip to Ukraine in February 2023, AllSides presented three articles that covered the news event. The articles represented viewpoints classified as center (Reuters), left (CNN), and right (Fox News). The Reuters article focused on the planning and secrecy of the visit. The CNN article described Biden's visit as "demonstrating in dramatic personal fashion his commitment to the country." The Fox News article noted the visit was Biden's first since Russia's invasion a year earlier.

Kevin Liptak, "Biden makes surprise visit to Ukraine for first time since full-scale war began," CNN.com. February 20 2023. www.cnn.com.

or listeners in a particular way. They can do this by choosing not to publish or broadcast specific stories or by minimizing or magnifying the importance of certain stories. News reporting can also influence reactions and thinking by not including certain information or perspectives or by suggesting that opinions or beliefs are objective facts. Slanted, or biased, news reporting often tells only one side of a story and makes little or no effort to obtain other views of the event or action. News reporting can also be used to attack an individual personally, rather than objectively reporting his or her position on an issue or event.

Media bias can also be the result of spin, which is the selling of a specific message that is heavily biased in favor of a particular point of view. Spin occurs when a journalist or news organization tries to create an eye-catching, memorable story through the use of unsubstantiated claims, sensational language, or shocking headlines. Often these tactics appear in attention-grabbing headlines that entice readers to click through to the content. Other times spin is more subtle, such as when a writer uses sensational or dramatic language instead of neutral word choices. For example, words such as *boasted*, *gloated*, *raged*, and *mocked* are used to stir emotions and can indicate bias.

Social Media Intensifies Bias

While media bias exists in traditional news reporting, social media can intensify it. Social media makes it easy to find and interact with like-minded people, which creates online echo chambers. In echo chambers, users frequently hear news and opinions that match their beliefs and viewpoints. And that makes it more likely that users will encounter and accept biased news reports on social media, because they share the same bias.

Social media algorithms select content to fill users' feeds based on what they have previously shown they liked. When a user clicks on news articles that support one side of an issue, the algorithm will promote similar information in that user's feed. Often, users do not realize they are seeing filtered information and not getting the entire

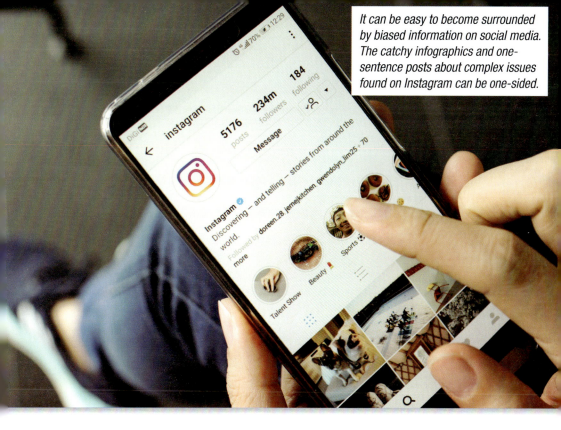

It can be easy to become surrounded by biased information on social media. The catchy infographics and one-sentence posts about complex issues found on Instagram can be one-sided.

picture. Users can become more biased when they only get part of the story and see little information that contradicts their views. They might believe that more people agree with their views than is true because they only see similar views on social media. As one becomes more biased, engaging with others who do not share the same ideas can also become more challenging.

Gracie Gilligan, a recent graduate of Maynard High School in Massachusetts, knows firsthand how easy it is to become surrounded by biased information on social media. Gilligan admits that Instagram was one of her primary information sources. She now realizes that the plethora of catchy infographics and one-sentence posts about complex issues were one-sided. The social media echo chamber spilled over into the real world for many of her peers. "A lot of my friends and my peers got really polarized at a very young age, and people were really angry at anyone who believed differently than them," she says. "And a lot of that came from having a very one-sided view of the issues that we were seeing."[44]

What's in a Name?

Not all websites and news sources are equally reliable and trustworthy. Many people believe that if a website has a .org domain name, it is more reliable than a .com website. However, that is not always true. Anyone can register for a website with a .org domain and use it. Also, .org domains are typically used by nonprofit organizations with the purpose of persuading rather than informing the public. Websites with a domain of .gov or .edu are usually credible information sources. These domains are reserved for government websites (.gov) and for colleges and universities (.edu). Instead of making an assumption based on a domain name, users need to investigate a source carefully, no matter what its name is.

Fighting Media Bias on Social Media

Recognizing and combating bias is becoming increasingly important as more people use social media platforms to access news and information. "If the companies and algorithms aren't doing it for us, it's up to us to regulate ourselves,"[45] says Jess Davis, a digital marketer specializing in the responsible use of technology.

One of the most straightforward strategies to resist bias is to cultivate a wide virtual network on social media. Following people with different perspectives and reading a variety of news outlets and sources can help users get out of an echo chamber and develop a more accurate picture of an issue. They can actively follow trustworthy publications that represent a variety of viewpoints. A social media feed that follows and engages with conservative and liberal news outlets will at least provide some balance and might avoid stories whose main purpose is to elicit anger rather than inform.

Another strategy to create a more balanced social media feed is to like content from all perspectives. Social media algorithms will have difficulty picking one-sided content for a user's feed if they cannot determine a user's preferences. Instead, the algorithm will show a mix of content as it keeps trying to learn the user's preferences. Also, some social media platforms allow users to change their account settings to see the most recent posts instead of personalized content, allowing more balanced content to appear in a feed.

Users should also pay attention to the accounts frequently appearing in their feeds. They may want to temporarily mute accounts that consistently feature biased content or share similar views with them. Doing so may allow new voices, accounts, and content to appear in social media feeds and bring new perspectives and information.

Identifying Bias

Reading, watching, or listening to news on social media does not have to be a passive activity. To identify bias, social media users can ask themselves questions such as, Who is the intended audience? Is the author an authority on this subject? Have any facts been left out of the content? A starting point to gather answers to these questions is to compare the information across multiple sources and platforms. If a story appears on Facebook, check to see how it is presented in national newspapers and other verified sources.

Users should also consider the purpose of the content and whether that purpose is clear. There is nothing wrong with opinionated content if it is clearly labeled as opinion or analysis. But news consumers should be wary of opinionated content that masquerades as fact. Inflammatory language and broad statements without supporting facts are signs of biased reporting. Checking a source's "About Us" page or mission statement can provide clues to its purpose in writing and why the source was created.

Changing How the World Gets News

Social media has changed the way the world gets its news. People worldwide have greater access to news and information than ever before, from anywhere, anytime. "It is important for us to recognize how much of an impact social media has had on

Some people say that more work needs to be done to teach people the skills they need to navigate news and information on social media. This librarian at a high school in Brookfield, Connecticut, teaches a required class on media literacy skills.

our reporting. There are strengths in it. There are ways to reach people that you couldn't reach before,"[46] says Melissa Bell, publisher of Vox Media.

Social media has removed many of the traditional gatekeepers to the news. Anyone with an internet-connected device can post news content with varying amounts of fact-checking and verification. Therefore, users need to become smarter consumers of news on social media. "We have to find ways to break through the clutter so that they get at the truth,"[47] says Kimberly Godwin, ABC News president.

Frank Baker is a journalist who works with school districts to improve media lit-

> "It is important for us to recognize how much of an impact social media has had on our reporting."[46]
>
> —Melissa Bell, publisher of Vox Media

eracy and social media literacy. He believes that more work needs to be done to teach people the skills they need to successfully navigate news and information on social media. He notes that

> social media is feeding into the obsession of satisfying people's need to have something quick. Unfortunately, that leads to superficiality. A headline or a tweet is only a summary—readers need to understand that there is always more to the story. There are many excellent sources of information, IF you know where to find it. And if readers will take the time to explore reliable and trustworthy sources.[48]

SOURCE NOTES

Introduction: Distributing News on TikTok

1. Quoted in Taylor Lorenz, "The White House Is Briefing TikTok Stars About the War in Ukraine," *Washington Post*, March 11, 2022. www.washingtonpost.com.
2. Quoted in Lorenz, "The White House Is Briefing TikTok Stars About the War in Ukraine."
3. Quoted in Lorenz, "The White House Is Briefing TikTok Stars About the War in Ukraine."
4. Quoted in Lorenz, "The White House Is Briefing TikTok Stars About the War in Ukraine."
5. Quoted in Simge Andi, "How and Why Do Consumers Access News on Social Media?," Reuters Institute, June 23, 2021. https://reutersinstitute.politics.ox.ac.uk.
6. Quoted in Andi, "How and Why Do Consumers Access News on Social Media?"

Chapter One: How People Get News

7. Quoted in Kat Tenbarge, "Floridians Are Livestreaming Hurricane Ian on TikTok," NBC News, September 28, 2022. www.nbcnews.com.
8. Quoted in Tenbarge, "Floridians Are Livestreaming Hurricane Ian on TikTok."
9. Quoted in Steven Potter, "How and Why Twitter Corrections Happen," Center for Journalism Ethics, University of Wisconsin–Madison, January 22, 2018. https://ethics.journalism.wisc.edu.
10. Quoted in Josh Lane, "Where Cutthroat Reporting Falls Short: False Reporting in Sports," *Daily Beacon* (Knoxville, TN), March 17, 2021. www.utdailybeacon.com.
11. Quoted in Taylor Lorenz, "Online Mobs Are Now Coming for Student Journalists," *Washington Post*, November 19, 2022. www.washingtonpost.com.
12. Quoted in Lorenz, "Online Mobs Are Now Coming for Student Journalists."
13. Margaret Sullivan, "Online Harassment of Female Journalists Is Real, and It's Increasingly Hard to Endure," *Washington Post*, March 14, 2021. www.washingtonpost.com.

Chapter Two: False and Misleading Information Goes Viral

14. Quoted in Ben Cost, "BBC Correspondent Falsely Reported Queen Died, Shocking Twitter," *New York Post*, September 8, 2022. https://nypost.com.
15. Quoted in Cost, "BBC Correspondent Falsely Reported Queen Died, Shocking Twitter."
16. Quoted in Cost, "BBC Correspondent Falsely Reported Queen Died, Shocking Twitter."
17. Quoted in Drew Desilver, "Q&A: Telling the Difference Between Factual and Opinion Statements in the News," Pew Research Center, June 18, 2018. www.pewresearch.org.
18. Quoted in Desilver, "Q&A."
19. Quoted in Desilver, "Q&A."
20. Paula Schuck, "My Teens Get Their News from TikTok, So I'm Fighting Misinformation with a Newspaper Subscription," CBC Parents, July 26, 2021. www.cbc.ca.
21. David Rand and Gordon Pennycock, "Most People Don't Actively Seek to Share Fake News," *Scientific American*, March 17, 2021. www.scientificamerican.com.
22. Quoted in Cara Rosenbloom, "Garlic and Bleach Won't Cure Coronavirus. How Such Myths Originated—and Why They're Wrong," *Washington Post*, March 10, 2020. www.washingtonpost.com.
23. Quoted in Marianna Spring, "The Human Cost of Virus Misinformation," BBC, May 27, 2020. www.bbc.com.
24. Marc Owen Jones, "Anatomy of a Disinformation Campaign: The Coup That Never Was," Al Jazeera, May 19, 2020. www.aljazeera.com.
25. Jones, "Anatomy of a Disinformation Campaign."

Chapter Three: Social Media Creates Echo Chambers

26. Marielle DeVos, "The Echo Chamber Effect: Social Media's Role in Political Bias," Institute for Youth in Policy, June 21, 2021. https://yipinstitute.org.
27. Quoted in Christopher Seneca, "How to Break Out of Your Social Media Echo Chamber," *Wired*, September 17, 2020. www.wired.com.
28. Quoted in Grese Sermaxhaj, "Echo Chambers and Its Effect on Different Social Media Platforms: An Interview with Walter Quattrociocchi," Youth Time Magazine, March 25, 2021. https://youthtimemag.com.
29. Quoted in Rani Molla, "Social Media Is Making a Bad Political Situation Worse," Vox, November 10, 2020. www.vox.com.
30. Quoted in Ari Shapiro et al., "How the Polarizing Effect of Social Media Is Speeding Up," NPR, September 9, 2022. www.npr.org.
31. Quoted in Shapiro et al., "How the Polarizing Effect of Social Media Is Speeding Up."

Chapter Four: Evaluating News Sources

32. Quoted in Carolyn Jabs, "Teaching Teens About News Bias and How to Find Reliable News Sources," Staten Island Parent, October 1, 2020. www.siparent.com.
33. Quoted in Mary Kate Lonergan, "What Is Media Literacy and How Can Simple Shifts Center It," *Teachers' Lounge* (blog), PBS, October 28, 2022. www.pbs.org.
34. Lonergan, "What Is Media Literacy and How Can Simple Shifts Center It."
35. Lonergan, "What Is Media Literacy and How Can Simple Shifts Center It."
36. Quoted in Tiffany Hsu, "When Teens Find Misinformation, These Teachers Are Ready," *New York Times*, September 8, 2022. www.nytimes.com.
37. Quoted in Jennifer Portorreal, "NJ Schools Would Teach Students Media Literacy to Discern Fact from Fiction Under New Bill," North Jersey.com, December 22, 2022. www.northjersey.com.
38. Quoted in Lex Merrell, "'Don't Believe Everything You Read': The Story of the Onion," *Bennington (VT) Banner*, September 30, 2022. www.benningtonbanner.com.
39. Quoted in University of Maryland College of Education, "Navigating Away from Online Misinformation," 2022. https://education.umd.edu.
40. Quoted in University of Maryland College of Education, "Navigating Away from Online Misinformation."
41. Quoted in James Rainey, "'Media Literacy' Advocates Push to Create Savvier Consumers of News and Information," *Los Angeles Times*, October 26, 2022. www.latimes.com.

Chapter Five: Recognizing Bias

42. Jacquelyn Whiting, "Everyone Has Invisible Bias. This Lesson Shows Students How to Recognize It," EdSurge, September 4, 2019. www.edsurge.com.
43. Whiting, "Everyone Has Invisible Bias."
44. Quoted in Hsu, "When Teens Find Misinformation, These Teachers Are Ready."
45. Quoted in Seneca, "How to Break Out of Your Social Media Echo Chamber."
46. Quoted in Greg Jones, "Journalists Give Thumbs Down to Social Media," Northwestern University Local News Initiative, February 9, 2022. https://localnewsinitiative.northwestern.edu.
47. Quoted in Jones, "Journalists Give Thumbs Down to Social Media."
48. Quoted in LCom Team, "Why Is Media Literacy in Education Important?," Learning.com, July 12, 2022. www.learning.com.

FOR FURTHER RESEARCH

Books

Kathryn Hulick, *Media Literacy: Information and Disinformation*. San Diego, CA: ReferencePoint, 2022.

Jennifer LaGarde and Darren Hudgins, *Developing Digital Detectives: Essential Lessons for Discerning Fact from Fiction in the "Fake News" Era*. Portland, OR: International Society for Technology in Education, 2021. Kindle.

Michael Miller, *Fake News: Separating Truth from Fiction*. Minneapolis, MN: Twenty-First Century, 2019.

Cindy L. Otis, *True or False: A CIA Analyst's Guide to Spotting Fake News*. New York: Square Fish, 2022.

Barbara Sheen, *The Fake News Crisis: How Misinformation Harms Society*. San Diego, CA: ReferencePoint, 2022.

Seema Yasmin, *What the Fact? Finding the Truth in All the Noise*. New York: Simon & Schuster Books for Young Readers, 2022.

Internet Sources

Ian Fox, "Don't Be Fooled by Fake Screenshots," Poynter Institute, November 21, 2022. www.poynter.org.

Taylor Lorenz, "The White House Is Briefing TikTok Stars About the War in Ukraine," *Washington Post*, March 11, 2022. www.washingtonpost.com.

Monmouth University, "Media Literacy & Misinformation: Evaluating Sources," December 15, 2022. https://guides.monmouth.edu.

Pew Research Center, "Many Americans Get News on YouTube, Where News Organizations and Independent Producers Thrive Side by Side," September 28, 2020. www.pewresearch.org.

Christopher Seneca, "How to Break Out of Your Social Media Echo Chamber," *Wired*, September 17, 2020. www.wired.com.

Websites

AllSides
www.allsides.com
AllSides is a website that evaluates the political bias of media reports. It presents different versions of similar news stories from different perspectives to help readers step outside of a filter bubble and see all sides of an issue or event.

FactCheck.org
www.factcheck.org
A project of the Annenberg Public Policy Center, FactCheck.org is a nonprofit website that aims to reduce the level of deception and confusion in US politics by providing original research on misinformation and hoaxes.

Media Literacy Now
https://medialiteracynow.org
Media Literacy Now is a nonprofit organization that aims to ensure all students are taught media literacy to they can become educated media consumers and creators.

MediaWise Teen Fact-Checking Network, Poynter Institute
www.poynter.org/mediawise/programs/tfcn
The Poynter Institute's MediaWise Teen Fact-Checking Network publishes fact-checks for teenagers—all done by teenagers. The site debunks misinformation and teaches users how to fact-check on their own.

News Literacy Project
https://newslit.org
The News Literacy Project works with educators and journalists to give students the skills they need to discern fact from fiction and to know what to trust.

INDEX

Note: Boldface page numbers indicate illustrations.

advertisers/advertisements and algorithms, 26, 29–30
age and use of social media platforms as news sources, 6
algorithms, **27**
   advertisers/advertisements and, 26, 29–30
   curation ability of social media platforms and, 26
   echo chambers and, 26, 29–31, 50–51, 52
   increase in user engagement with social media as goal of, 34, 47
   information missed by users and, 32
   news covered on social media platforms and, 16
AllSides, 49
alternative social media platforms, 15
Annenberg Public Policy Center, 42

Babylon Bee (satiric website), 40
Baker, Frank, 53–54
Bauer, Trevor, 12–13, **13**
Bell, Melissa, 52–53
bias, 47–49
   See also media bias
bias confirmation trap, 47–48
Biden, Joe
   coverage of trip to Ukraine by, 49
   State of the Union address by (2023), 42
   TikTok influencers and, 4, 5–6
Blakesley, Paul, 38
businesses on social media platforms, 9

Casieri, Gabrielle, 37–38
citizen journalists, 11
clickbait articles, 41
Colorado, 22–24
confirmation bias and echo chambers, 27–28
Conversation (nonprofit online news organization), 39–40
COVID-19, **22**, **28**
   echo chambers during pandemic, 28–29
   misinformation about, on social media, 11, 22–24
   verifying information about vaccine for, 44

Davis, Jess, 52
democracy
   misinformation's effect on, 24
   polarization of society and, 31, 32–33, **33**
Dikkers, Scott, 41
disinformation, 24–25, 41–42
domain names, 52

echo chambers
   algorithms and, 26, 29–31, 50–51, 52
   basic facts about, 27, 29, 31
   confirmation bias and, 27–28
   COVID-19 and, 28–29
   democracy and, 31, 32–33, **33**
   filter bubble, 29–31
   getting out of, 52–53
   incomplete information and, 32
Elizabeth (queen of England), 17–18, **18**
explicit bias, 47, 49
exposure effect, 29

Facebook
   filter bubbles and, 30
   misinformation about COVID-19 on, 23
   polarization of political views and, 31
fact-checking, 42, 44–45, 49
FactCheck.org, 42
filter bubbles, 29–31
Finkel, Eli, 33
Fisher, Max, 33, 34
Flaherty, Rob, 4

Gab and filter bubbles, 30
Garrison, Cassandra, 12
Gentzkow, Matthew, 31

Gen-Z for Change, 5
Gilligan, Gracie, 51
Godwin, Kimberly, 53
Goff, Teddy, 6
Greene, Kahlil, 5
Gregory, Jamie, 43–44

Hakim, Yalda, 17, 18
harassment of journalists, 14–15
Hitchens, Brian Lee, 23–24
Hitchens, Erin, 23–24
Hurricane Ian, 11

implicit bias, 47
influencers
    Biden administration and, 4, 5–6
    as White House correspondents for Gen Z, 6
Instagram, 51

Jones, Marc Owen, 25
journalists
    bias and, 48, **48**, 49
    on social media platforms, 9–10
        absence of vetting information of, 32
        anyone with account as, 11
        control over stories by, 15–16
        harassment of, 14–15
        and relationship with public, 14
    traditional, 8, **9**
        control over stories by, 15
        harassment on social media of, 14–15

Krupp, Olivia, 14

lateral reading, 42–44
Lonergan, Mary Kate, 37

McGrew, Sarah, 43
McRaney, David, 28
media bias
    checking for, 49
    effects of, **48**, 48–49
    intensified by social media, 50–51, **52**
    strategies to resist, 52–53
    types of, 49–50
media literacy
    clickbait articles and, 41
    confirming details and, 44–45
    defining, 37
    evaluating articles' sources and, 38–39

    false, misleading, or out-of-context photos and, 45–46
    importance of, 37
    lateral reading and, 42–44
    purpose served by content and, 45
    recognizing satire and, 39–41, **40**
    verifying information and, 44
misinformation
    about COVID-19, **22**, 22–24
    absence of vetting information on social media and, 32, 35
    on alternative social media platforms, 15
    consequences of, 24
    on larger, more established social media platforms, 11, 17–18
    opinions mistaken for facts and, 18–21, **20**
    on TikTok, 11
Mitchell, Amy, on inability to distinguish opinion from fact, 19, 20, 21

National Association for Media Literacy Education, 37
NewsGuard, 11
news outlets, traditional
    basic facts about, 8, **9**
    bias and, 48, **48**, 49
    control over stories by journalists and editors of, 15
    harassment of journalists on social media and, 14–15
    opinion versus fact in, 18–19
    on social media platforms, 9–10
news outlets on social media platforms
    absence of labels separating opinion from fact, 19, **20**
    accuracy of, 19
        absence of vetting information and, 32, 35
        disinformation and, 41–42
        false, misleading, or out-of-context photos and, 45–46
        incomplete or one-sided information and, 41
        purpose served by content and, 45
    age of users of, 6
    algorithms and likes determine news covered by, 16
    basic facts about, 9
    checking for bias in, 49
    clickbait articles from, 41
    evaluating sources of, 38–39
    fact-checking, 42, 44–45

    lateral reading and, 42–44
    media bias intensified by, 50–51, **52**
    most popular sites for, 6
    in real time, 11–13, 55
    satire on, 39–41, **40**
    smartphones and, 9, **10**
    strengths of, 52–53
    traditional, 9–10
    young adults as consumers of, 6, 36, **36**
    See also under journalists
Nightengale, Bob, 13

Onion (satiric website), **40**, 40–41

Pennycock, Gordon, 22
personal bias, 47
Pew Research Center
    on ability to distinguish opinion from fact on social media, 20–21
    on American use of social media platforms, 8–9
    as source of news, 11
    on job-related harassment or threats of journalists on social media, 15
    on one-sided information on social media platforms, 41
    on use of alternative social media platforms, 15
    on use of social media platforms as news sources, 6
photos, false, misleading, or out-of-context, 45–46
PolitiFact, 42
Psaki, Jen, 4

Qatar, disinformation about, 24–25
Quattrociocchi, Walter, 30

Rand, David, 22
Reddit and filter bubbles, 30
Reuters Institute, 7
reverse image searches, 46

Sanders, Sarah Huckabee, 42
Sapienza University of Rome, 30
satire, 39–41, **40**
Schuck, Paula, 21
Sharkawy, Abdu, 23
smartphones, social media platforms and, 9, **10**
social media platforms
    alternative, 15

    businesses on, 9
    curation ability of, 26
    as echo chambers, 16
    format of, 22
    increase in use of (2005–2023), 8–9
    increase in user engagement as goal of, 34, 47
    polarization of society and, 31, 32–33, **33**
    potential of, to spread information rapidly, 23
    volume of content on, 21–22
spin, described, 50
Stanford University, 43
Stecklein, Brad, 11
stereotypes and bias, 47
Sullivan, Margaret, 15

TikTok
    basic facts about, 4
    Hurricane Ian on, 11
    misinformation on, 11
    as news source, 4–5, **5**
Turning Point USA, 45–46
Twitter
    disinformation on, 24–25
    filter bubbles and, 30
    misinformation on, 17–18
    as source of breaking news, 7

Ukraine-Russia conflict, White House briefing of influencers about, 4, 5
unconscious bias, 47, 49
University of Chicago Pearson Institute/AP-NORC, 24
University of Regina (Canada), 19, 22

websites, domain names of, 52
Whiting, Jacquelyn, 48

YikYak, 14
young adults
    as consumers of news on social media, 6, 36, **36**
    lateral reading and ability to identify unreliable information by, 43–44
    as White House correspondents for Gen Z, 6
YouTube, misinformation about COVID-19 on, 23

Zeiler, Ellie, 6
Zublick, David, 23

PICTURE CREDITS

Cover: Vasya Kobelev/Shutterstock.com

5: Butsaya/Shutterstock.com

9: Gorodenkoff/Shutterstock.com

10: Cristian Dina/Shutterstock.com

13: Cal Sport Media/Alamy Stock Photo

18: Salma Bashir Motiwala/Shutterstock.com

20: Pheelings media/Shutterstock.com

22: Ringo Chiu/Shutterstock.com

27: sitthiphong/Shutterstock.com

28: Pordee_Aomboon/Shutterstock.com

33: Daniel Krason/Shutterstock.com

36: fizkes/Shutterstock.com

40: NetPhotos/Alamy Stock Photo

45: Salma Bashir Motiwala/Shutterstock.com

48: BAZA Production/Shutterstock.com

51: AngieYeoh/Shutterstock.com

54: Associated Press